A World of Field Trips

Going to a Zoo

Rebecca Rissman

D0537884

Raintree

I2589268

www.raintreepublishers.co.uk
Visit our website to find out
more information about
Raintree books.

To order:
☎ Phone 0845 6044371
🖨 Fax +44 (0) 1865 312263
🖳 Email myorders@raintreepublishers.co.uk

Customers from outside the UK please telephone +44 1865 312262

Raintree is an imprint of Capstone Global Library Limited, a company incorporated in England and Wales having its registered office at 7 Pilgrim Street, London, EC4V 6LB – Registered company number: 6695582.

Edited by Rebecca Rissman, Dan Nunn, and Catherine Veitch
Designed by Richard Parker
Picture research by Tracy Cummins
Originated by Capstone Global Library Ltd
Printed and bound in China by Leo Paper Products Ltd

ISBN 978 1 406 23521 0 (hardback)
16 15 14 13 12 11
10 9 8 7 6 5 4 3 2 1

ISBN 978 1 406 23530 2 (paperback)
17 16 15 14 13 12
10 9 8 7 6 5 4 3 2 1

British Library Cataloguing in Publication Data
Rissman, Rebecca.
Going to a zoo. -- (World of field trips)
590.7'3-dc22

Acknowledgements
We would like to thank the following for permission to reproduce photographs: AP Photo p. 9 (Franka Bruns); Corbis pp. 4 (© Vstock LLC/Tetra Images), 7 (© KIM KYUNG-HOON/Reuters), 8 (© BEAWIHARTA/Reuters), 14 (© Martin Harvey), 16 (© Gail Mooney), 23b (© Martin Harvey), 23d (© BEAWIHARTA/Reuters); Getty Images pp. 5 (ROBERT FRANCOIS/AFP/), 6 (Engel & Gielen), 10 (Image Source), 13 (Koichi Kamoshid), 15 (Ghislain & Marie David de Lossy), 20 (Purestock); Photolibrary p. 19 (Photodisc); Shutterstock pp. 11 (© vblinov), 12 (© Mircea BEZERGHEANU), 17 (© Taras Vyshnya), 18 (© Elena Elisseeva), 21 (© Hallgerd), 22 (© tororo reaction), 23a (© Mircea BEZERGHEANU), 23c (© vblinov).

Front cover photograph of tourists playing with elephants at Mae Sa elephant camp in Chiang Mai province, Thailand reproduced with permission of Getty Images (PORNCHAI KITTIWONGSAKUL/AFP). Back cover photograph of children stroking a llama reproduced with permission of Shutterstock (© vblinov).

Every effort has been made to contact copyright holders of any material reproduced in this book. Any omissions will be rectified in subsequent printings if notice is given to the publisher.

Contents

Field trips

People go on field trips to visit new places.

People go on field trips to learn
new things.

Field trip to a zoo

Some people go on field trips to zoos.

A zoo is a place where people can see different animals.

Zookeepers work at zoos.

Zookeepers care for the animals.

Zookeepers teach people about the animals.

Different zoos

This is a petting zoo.

You can touch the animals here.

This is an aquarium.

You can see underwater
animals here.

This is a wildlife reserve.

You can see animals living in the
wild here.

This is a city zoo.

The zoo is near the city.

This is a bird park.

You can see different types of birds here.

How should you behave at a zoo?

You should not feed the animals at a zoo.

You should not put your hand through the fences.

What do you think?

What kind of zoo is this?

Look on page 24 for the answer.

Picture glossary

aquarium special place where many underwater animals are kept

reserve special place for wild animals

zoo place where different animals are kept

zookeeper person who cares for animals living in a zoo

Index

Notes for parents and teachers

Before reading
Explain to children that a field trip is a short visit to a new place, and that it often takes place during a school day. Ask children if they have ever taken a field trip. Tell pupils that a zoo is a special place where animals are kept. People can visit the zoo to see the animals and learn about nature.

After reading
- Tell children that there are many types of zoos. Ask children to draw a poster for one type of zoo. It could be a bird park, an aquarium, or a zoo that contains many different animals. Display the posters around the room.

Answer to page 22
It is an aquarium.